Other Books by Marc Vincenz

Poetry

The Propaganda Factory, or Speaking of Trees
Mao's Mole
Gods of a Ransacked Century
Behind the Wall at the Sugar Works (a verse novel)
Beautiful Rush
Additional Breathing Exercises
This Wasted Land and Its Chymical Illuminations (annotated by Tom Bradley)
Becoming the Sound of Bees
Sibylline (illustrated by Dennis Paul Williams)
The Syndicate of Water & Light
Leaning into the Infinite
Here Comes the Nightdust
Einstein Fledermaus
The Little Book of Earthly Delights
A Brief Conversation with Consciousness (illustrated by Sophia Santos)
There Might Be a Moon or a Dog
39 Wonders and Other Management Issues
The Pearl Diver of Irunmani
A Splash of Cave Paint
The King of Prussia is Drunk on Stars
Spells for the Wicked (illustrated by Sophia Santos and Jake Quatt)
IRØNCLAD (illustrated by Jake Quatt)
No More Animal Poems
Mythodology
The Form of Time: New and Selected Poems

Limited Editions and Chapbooks

Benny and the Scottish Blues (illustrated by Darene Dewan)
Genetic Fires
Upholding Half the Sky
Pull of the Gravitons
An Alphabet of Last Rites
The Mayfly Codex

Three Telltale Love Signs
Rocketship to the Andromeda Galaxy
Faery Ecology (illustrated by Sophia Santos)

Translations

Kissing Nests by Werner Lutz
Nightshift / An Area of Shadows by Erika Burkart and Ernst Halter
A Late Recognition of the Signs by Erika Burkart
Grass Grows Inward by Andreas Neeser
Out of the Dust by Klaus Merz
Secret Letter by Erika Burkart
Lifelong Bird Migration by Jürg Amann
Unexpected Development by Klaus Merz
An Audible Blue: Selected Poems (1963–2016) by Klaus Merz
Casting a Spell in Spring by Alexander Xaver Gwerder
Country of Small Men by Ernst Halter
In the House, Still Light by Klaus Merz
Mother's Letters, Pure Caviar: Selected Poems by Ion Monoran
       translated with Marius Surleac
Dreaming Jack by Klaus Merz

Fiction

The Visitation
City of Lemons
Three Taos of Tao, or How to Catch an Ivory Elephant
Station H_2O

Graphic Novel

Coalition No. 9 (illustrated by Jake Quatt)

PRAISE for *ALL THE TRICKS OF LANGUAGE*

The first thing to occur to me upon reading *All the Tricks of Language* is wanting to go back and read each poem again, and again, and again, because it felt so good. The words clicked into place like the gears of a clock, sonic subtleties combined with the vivid, tactile imagery of a *theatrum mundi*. This is the work of a seasoned poet, with a bit of the bricklayer in him. Phanopoeia spread with a trowel. Flashes of linguistic splendor, tastefully muted by an overarching sense of decorum, illumine particularities of truth, the manifest beauty of things in themselves 'tricked into breathing.'   —JOHN OLSON

All The Tricks of Language—that title glitters, disappears into itself, and ushers in a wild and meticulous poetics of forward motion. Vincenz is a dancemaster who understands that we exist against terrific odds. There's a chord of tears and laughter, an intimate knowledge of our vulnerability: 'the sinful and awkward under the lion's gaze'. The architecture of this book is vertiginous. Background becomes foreground ('the disciples will tell you it wasn't a bad supper'), foreground is open to the night sky ('the absolute demand/yet more...'). Vincenz has a dazzling wit and a great eye for the contingent, the perishable, the hue of a damselfly's eye. *All The Tricks Of Language* is a book like no other—a bravura tour de force. a *sui generis* structure, a volley of arrows shot into the unknown.   —D. NURKSE

Marc Vincenz has done it again! In *All the Tricks of Language*, he gives his readers a hybrid wonder.... A play starring Denise Levertov and Sylvia Plath and Pessoa and John Donne. A lyric suite. A pastiche. An epic complete with a descent into the Underworld. A prayer for all the sentient beings on this planet. An ode to our pipes and man made marvels. *All the Tricks of Language* is a remarkable feat from an assiduous wordsmith who builds a world like no other.   —DENISE DUHAMEL

Marc Vincenz's *All the Tricks of Language* conjures a panoply of sentient beings, including—yet not excluding—the Norse god Freyr, Fernando Pessoa, and torpor trapped beneath fish scales. These poems journey across space and time, through and under plants and planets, and into variations of life forms. Concurrently, the poems sing to beloved ghosts and dreamers, and, extraordinarily, the poet collects the echoes of these ghosts, offering them, too, to us. Such magical worlds materialize through the curtain of the poet's material, which is language, due to his sheer virtuosity. —MARTINE BELLEN

With *All the Tricks of Language*, Marc Vincenz has indeed mastered all the tricks: lyric, rhetorical, metaphoric, 'the tinkle of irony,' drama, comedy—pages filled with people starry as themselves, meeting here on the other side of history as well as this side: 'the world intertwined with the unworld', 'an ocean of unimaginable secrets.' *All the Tricks of Language* is fertile and carnivalesque, grabbing your attention from the very start. Vincenz writes like no one else, vitally original with, perhaps Stevens, Pound, Kafka, and Calvino in the background, along with a handful of Language poets.

 Words and phrases bubble up from a magma, forming a molted coherence, a dynamic structure, a natural order. The meaning Vincenz creates is as far from prose reduction as possible, making for 'a provision of epiphanies'. Language itself is a realm, where narrative digs in and picks up. People float up and fade, rise elsewhere. Indeed, 'if we were following all the rules of scripture, by now all would be dead.' Instead, all is very much alive. The scripture created is deeply ironic while engaged at the same time. Irony creates continuity, new meanings and forms to carry them, a kind of Hegelian dialectic: 'there's more to the story than that.'

 The mind, for example, in the poem, "In a History of Half-light," works in the quotidian, translating, transforming, thus making it more of itself. This is a dynamic, gnomic world, a full-bodied manifesto: 'Everything which is transforming/will continue.' I am convinced from the beginning, and, 'follow the carrot in [in the poet's] hand'. The only stick there is, in the manner of the Zen master, is a sharp tap to the side of the head: Wake up!

A deeply impressive, engaging, supremely original work of art.

—BRIAN SWANN

ALL
THE TRICKS
OF LANGUAGE

MARC VINCENZ

DOS MADRES

2025

DOS MADRES PRESS INC.

P.O. Box 294, Loveland, Ohio 45140
www.dosmadres.com   editor@dosmadres.com

Dos Madres is dedicated to the belief that the small press is essential to the vitality of contemporary literature as a carrier of the new voice, as well as the older, sometimes forgotten voices of the past. And in an ever more virtual world, to the creation of fine books pleasing to the eye and hand.

Dos Madres is named in honor of Vera Murphy and Libbie Hughes, the "Dos Madres" whose contributions have made this press possible.

Dos Madres Press, Inc. is an Ohio Not For Profit Corporation and a 501 (c) (3) qualified public charity. Contributions are tax deductible.

Executive Editor: Robert J. Murphy

Illustration & Book Design: Elizabeth H. Murphy
www.illusionstudios.net

Cover design by Marc Vincenz
Cover Illustration: "Homo Homunculus," by Sophia Santos
Interior illustrations: Marc Vincenz and Sophia Santos

Typeset in Adobe Garamond Pro & Century Gothic
ISBN 978-1-962847-33-9
Library of Congress Control Number: 2025943588

First Edition

for Enzo Fabrizi "Tricolore," bricklayer

featuring a cast of characters, including but not limited to
the various incarnations thereof:

Starring *Enzo Fabrizi "Tricolore"* as himself

Co-starring *Denise Priscilla Levertov,* with a cast of
thousands, as incarnations of themselves, including

The wrens and their evening river
John Donne
Time and soot and an empty wave
Tutankhamun
The sugar in nighttime
Fernando António Nogueira Pessoa
Emily Dickinson
Sylvia Plath
Leonard Nimoy
Julius Caesar
Horus
The grass looking for the honeybees
The great deeders
Harry Crosby and Ben Mazer
Torpor trapped beneath fish scales
An eye reflecting unborn miles
Mary Shelley
Seven "other" Sun gods
A bench above the ocean
A strange creature, half-man, half-air
William Shakespeare
Ox-Head and Horse-Face
Water Living in a Clock
The Greek gods, the Roman gods, and the Norse gods

A Spectacular Extravanganza Extraordinaire!!!

May we all meet there, on the other side of history.

TABLE OF CONTENTS

INTO THE DINING ROOM

OVER THE DRAWBRIDGE AND FAR AWAY

ONLY HALF AN HOUR FURTHER

A VERY MESSY AFFAIR

HOMUNCULUS CONTINUOUS

SEVEN SUN GODS

MEANWHILE ... ON THIRTEEN OTHER PLANETS

ALL
THE TRICKS
OF LANGUAGE

Last night
as if death had lit a pale light
in your flesh, your flesh
was cold to my touch, or not cold
but cool, cooling, as if the last traces
of warmth were still fading in you.
My thigh burned in cold fear where
yours touched it.

—Denise Levertov, from "Clouds"

Sono chiaramente
uno sciocco,
ma so come aggirare
il mortaio, martello
e il mattone.

— Enzo Fabrizi, carved with his trowel

INTO THE DINING ROOM

Hardwired into the Cogwork

There is hook in every benefit, that sticks in his jaws
that takes that benefit, and draws him
whither the benefactor will.

I. *Rules of Scripture*

A foregone conclusion?
Dead benefactor, you say?
Be aware, be plump, be sharp-eyed.

If you were following
all the rules of scripture,
by now we'd all be dead.

II. *One Sun Seen in Another*

Down in the pastures,
those having never seen
the light, the dust-eaters,

earth-tumblers, pressed
upon the mouth
of the cold glare:

all those shadows, edges, arches,
anything emerging from
time and soot everywhere.

III. *Into the Wormhole*

Watch the leaf in the sun
with your name on it tremble,
watch it spin, watch it

follow the journeys
of the day birds and
the night birds, hidden

in the deepest recesses
of the cell; watch
the quiet pendulum return.

How Do You Testify?

(1)

Staggering feats. Sweeping features. Sleeping figures. Silent movements, fetishes, undying wind …

(2)

A trickle of pity, a hidden mountain peak, porcupines in your sleep, the sugar in nighttime, the black that binds you to me, the as-and-when, that ditch of pickpockets, the lightning on a fuse, the long lashes of your look, the rocks that climb out of the sea, the fish on the shores of Galilee, the undying vision, the empty wave.

(3)

Hold that empty wave silently sweeping, the ascendant in ascendance, the staggering numbers, the singer in half-time.

(4)

How the trickle of pity unfolds, how the decadence of liturgy is a bitter taste of blood; or, fishing deep, the vermin streaks and you at the threshold, all those sweeping features, all the rocks that climb out of the sea, all the thieves clinging to the peaks.

In a History of Half-Light

In all these measures,
in the fields, across the treetops,
into the crag and bluster,
the muscled-in, the go-without,

it goes without saying:
it's easier to love fragments,
those scattered confections of a journey.
From the coast you can see the flashes

and etchings; and how you whisper
to the water in the evening river.
How marvelous too,
the sound of the bees

on their way to making honey.
In the anointed hours
when Dirt pricks up her ears
and a pigeon is caught in a snare,

the grapes ripen and the sky nests;
the birds loosen and the sun runs
into her depressions, into the sewers
or deep into the earth,

glazed over in pitch. And the nettles
and the sunflowers harken on wings
of insects who meet on the black thorn crowns
where the sea-green pupils

of the damselfly stare straight
through the dark, honing in
on those intervals of a third,
the dance of fire, and the wrens

in the marshgrass
flow-less in their seesaw,
painting inscriptions
on the rocks by the river

before their leaving,
never to return;
and the spark
that flooded the ashes

in all these measures,
enters the hive
with wings full of pollen
and an idea of ...

Down in Startime

You'd think she'd remember all of this from the first time.

If you believe all the questions
that arise from above—
the crimson-breasted god-queen stares down

in all her mercy—know
that everything fades out too,
even these moments on the prow across the pier;

know that history changes nothing,
everything which is transforming
and will continue … all those infernal questions;

and, in your form, one of the living few;
yes, you protrude, grazing my shoulder,
a leaking light—and the clock hands expand

as if they were those of another startime,

a single groove on the thin line
on a paper-cut moon, a childhood rewind—
memories from the deep siesta, the message

that has been carried on, the tales
of strange creatures like moray eels
spinning into their tails, the boundless

herring, a storm of mackerel darting through
shattered beams of ancient trawlers and fishing vessels,
of cargo ships laden with amphorae—olive, honey

and wine, casks of salt or bolts of silk, beeswax
and twine, and treasures from the secret cellars of Mycenae,
jewels too; or, in fact, the flesh

of wounded spring lambs,
a pandemonium of flavors,
everything that descended vicariously—

and all those trade winds headed southeast,
deep into the backcountry, into the rockbeds
and into the feathers of a dodo—

see, she is transfixed,
she wishes she had the wings
to whisk herself away.

Phases of the Moon

And it keeps blowing, and the footsteps go on …

It isn't over until you walk into the enclosed
garden, until the haze on the shore settles.

Melancholy, solitary, impenetrable, that laureled

poet swallowed by the blue as the wind plays
intently and ice thaws, and when the rain dies,

it will enfold you, lead you to some new adventure.

Twenty autumns hence, unafraid against
a background of pearl, the world solidifies,

and a breath, unheard, arrives on silver

fingers on deserted shores. The night,
ahead in all her glory, teems with life,

wisps of grass beat against time and,

in the river, the paddle wheels. Each winter
we shudder, drying our toes by the fire,

the sheen on the sills, all that loot and

plunder of summer slipping away, dripping
into the river below like mottled dragonfly wings.

Sometime in the Eighteenth Dynasty

*After clearing 9 metres of the descending passage, in about
the middle of the afternoon, we came upon a second sealed
doorway, which was almost the exact replica of the first.*

In the zigzag of the monkey-puzzle tree,
the twisted globes appear to touch
the light on the hills, and the gilded

thread of laundry lines glimmers
amongst the gutters. We venture out
into a whirlpool of waving hands.

Somewhere buried beneath this chamber
lies a woman once named Delilah.
Somehow, you still hear the solemn litany, feel

the children's fingers tugging at shirttails,
or perhaps some other ancient crime,
like climbing sheer walls in broad daylight,

or the Spanish tomatoes in the Egyptian greenhouse
tricked into breathing. Walk up
into the brightening pasture, the shepherds say.

Cross the Milky Way
on backs of dragons, the shaman say.
An old pharaoh once told me

it was best to die aroused.
When Time finally comes around,
you don't want to dilly-dally, he said.

At that moment I believed him—
in the sputter of the hieroglyphic rain,
it seemed so bloody convincing.

A Meeting on Waterways

It seems that all the light of morning has descended here, where it's usually dark, and the sputtering of frogs, bobbing their heads in the bulrushes, swarms among the oaks.

Weighing these few scraps, the things you've said you leapt gardens to procure—there are still more feathers on this side—hard work: all that feather versus fodder.

Tomorrow—what a difficult word—interrupted and intercepted; and tomorrow, all that we imagine.

Careful.

The universe has ears.

The Bread of Life

You have to come to the shore. There are no instructions.

I. *A Stone's Throw*

For Denise in her shadow, follow the veins
in her arms; at the river they gather and all
the stones return to life. Less manifest

than now, more a sign leading us where
the crystal refracts, with that something

that becomes divine; oh yes, we are so easily
appeased. With that spirit at your shoulder,
how could you ever be at anyone's mercy?

Meaning meaning could be composed
of virtually anything; but we want the bells

to resound through the foundations. What god
has a chance under conditions like that?
Watch for tarantulas here, they sneak through

the muddy creeks foreshadowing the storms, and yet,
they always declare: I am ready! Your fingers

hold the last fragment. Beyond the forest,
the fragile architecture peters out: pathways,
shadows, trestles, and trusses. Oh, the spores

of the once-possible, a mushroom says.
Lay your hands on the Atlantic Ocean and

feel how the trickle of compassion enters in.
(And yes, the hedgehogs here are particularly
spiny.) Together we could face the storm,

and right here in the threshold—think of it
threefold: you could lend me your face or,

if you were her, you'd be clutching the corals,
turning in your sixty-year-old heart
for a new sun and wake up to the droning

of time or that dizzy plunging into
a bowl of reflections. Consider this:

across the rooftops, you appear in the fire—
not wildly struggling—down in the shade
under a walnut tree. As you reflect, the fish

sink into the wake of emergency.
All those valleys and ravines, the enormous

howl from dawn to dawn—in the awnings,
in all the architecture, every gesture
appears and then disappears without a trace.

II. *Refractions*

For Denise, the crystal
refracts with that something
of virtually anything;
but we want the bells,
they always declare:
[Je suis prêt!]

Lay your hands
in the Atlantic Ocean;
and threefold: you
could lend me your face,
or, a cherry bowl of reflections;
consider this:

in all those valleys and ravines:
the enormous appears
and disappears
without a trace.

Endorsed but Not Elected

In fact[,] it's time to drill, baby, drill down.

All those sworn statements:
a massacre of silly geese—
think what occurs beneath

the words, never mind
the aftermath: the eagle
always stalks the mouse,

the faintest blur across the fields
clearly means something.
Crazy, but my thinking

is such that my lips don't find
the words. Honestly, I don't know
who you are—

there are all these variations
of yourself, there is some sort of
token recognition each time

the infallible sixth sense kicks in;
and you're myopic like that bug
that crawls up my arm

or the Davidoff cigars
that light up the chamber;
so halting, so tactless,

that way of seeing, and the pain
and the anguish, the pin in the gut,
that jabbering of antibiotics.

What's written is written,
but that doesn't mean it's true.
Do you think we are that unaware,

imagining only we and our beloved ones
are left here unblemished, unheard of,
living in the shade of the longest form?

The sky is so wide and clear tonight.

Here's a memo with all the talking points.

Heady Stuff

What do you mean you guess?

All those endless dedications, the paintings cramming the cellar, perhaps we'll never know.

Improbable, you said.

This, you said, is disaster enough. Dig in your heels, history is brief.

And then, all those disguises, you said. If man, is history may he remain wrapped in his shroud.

The quantitative leap into the beyond is less providential than preferential.

A Compulsive Moment

Your passage through the centuries, a voice blossoming—
and words falling lightly. Just a few minutes more and
you'll be lighting the lamps.

No, he wasn't expecting to see me, but I have arrived, my
angel, she said. This from the woman who had you on your
word. The word was defeat, perhaps? Or, that little nugget
of faith that clings on?

Drop me here, you said in the pouring rain, in the sky's
nest. Our life was once theirs. If only I had some blank
beach, you said, that I may draw these prayers into motion.
And all our troubles will be set in the sand.

Watch out for the beach umbrellas, you said, navigating
your way between strollers, sailors, and several other
Sagittariuses.

In the Dining Room

As sayings go, this one takes the ticket.

There's always a provider of epiphanies. Who but the priest or the wizard, or that impudent brat with his lucky gaffe.

Think on it in your own skyscraper, in the anteater's vast chambers, at the wedding or the funeral, in the Institute of Radiology, or during the pardoning of the prisoners, in your own regaled reality, really.

A drizzle outside and you're shuffling the cards. Rummage in your basket, offer me the very last shriveled fig. I know you're unaware of the fact that this dead man is his own man.

As the world's crust closes over, know this is no final goodbye—it costs too much. Yes, I hear them wailing hungrily. It's growing cold among the pyres. I know you shudder.

Honestly, I don't know what persists.

OVER THE DRAWBRIDGE AND FAR AWAY

It Was Only Half-Past Four

And the café was full—what wasn't talked about?

The ghastly heat, the dreadful shitting pigeons with their weirdly bulbous eyes, and the eczema that followed, a few spots of blood, or those stickers that read:

To be continued.

A Tribute to Whom

Oh, you genius, you beehive,
you spark, you contiguous line—
all from the same place of origin

where there is no breeze.

All those questions posed ...
take no notice, the image
is stamped on your brow, even

as you glare in the mirror,

as the others are orbiting,
the day is melting—and yes,
we tried, in the smoke, lounging

on the divan, to ask for both.

How could we grasp
your learned teachings? You lived
on the other side of the wall.

Your postal system isn't working.

Bring out the best glasses,
decant, pull out your moth-
eaten clothwares—the ones ravished

by life. You know you know the man

you bought them from.

Back in Town the Crow Bellows

Married young on the hemlines of celestials,
hatched from a single Venetian egg.

But, as the nymphs will tell you, spring
doesn't shine for long. Now it seems too late—

all those trollish gestures and yawls have
emerged from beneath the lanterns and lintels,

and the telephones jangling the news
of fates killed on highways is measured

in dead squirrels or grains of rice.
An old blackbird caws somewhere.

There is light to be had, she says. Look at
all that dirty crockery piled on the table—

or that deep view from the inside:
a long microscope pointing into credibility.

In Those Wily Old Ways

Dear Denise,
Above, but below
for those in the know, don't

listen to rumors; much
of the news has yet
to be delivered.

In the dark and early hours,
the wind ticks, and the wee
perfume separates

in the thread and weave
of those lounging chairs.
In the packs of clouds,

and in they-who-created-
many, multitudes,
a plentitude of questions.

Whether you know it
or not, gratitude
is no fool; she sifts

adroitly through
the garbage, across
islands and lakes …

or by the nature
of all these exclusions,
with this letter, I thee wed.

With the Weight of These Exclusions

No, I don't envy you either, you're so masked—you revert to biblical pauperism, and yet, you are the earth I love. I don't remember you in the armchair, whether it was a dream or not, whether you were channeling spirits, or maybe it was our four feet pounding out the weight of the dead. No, I wasn't indifferent, all your accomplices said too much; in their case, living or dead, it doesn't matter; either way, they were scrambling, fumbling, tugging at strings and threads.

Too much light from the nothingness, I say, when audible.

A Fruitful Purpose

All those fingerprints
have become extinct,

a future tense is missing—
look into the shadows.

Our journey has just begun,
let the invisible ones

guide us—*you* never removed
the hook from your chin.

And the blowing of the tornado
cutting up the coast, even though

the clock remains firm.
You can't be half-clocked, you'd said.

I renounce time, I'd said,
no doubt showing my outline,

wishing you might read my horo-
scope, darling. Whether where

we were was relevant, I'll leave up
to you. A singular birth says it all.

Memory or Recollection?

I. *Memory*

Daisies in your hair, grains of sand in your toes;
what an aristocratic house you come from!
The coast guard dusted off his arm every time

you passed. There's more to the story than

meets the eye, it goes on ad infinitum. I never
wanted to speak badly of you, but you were
in the dark about living, sacramental almost:

it was something unrealized, like that antelope

sparking off stones just outside Cape Town,
or the divisive act that probably led us here
in the first place. We were born to hide, not

running; unequipped in all our machinations …

tough medicine can be hard to swallow, still,
the miracle is all in you. Don't stand
on your pedestal of dictionaries, splay yourself

across the world. I know it's possibly too much

to bear. And that season of mine all wound up
in its own apparitions … Somewhere in India
we crossed a border, a thin veil of nothingness,

but I swear it was there in the all-seen and

the less-seen. Money or redemption?, you said, turning
over a new leaf in that winded myth.
The answer grows not in the wind but between

the boughs. So strategic you were, even when mostly
present or moaning about the past in the present;
yet all severed now, and outside, outside,

the hoot of the screech owls awakens me.

II. *Recollection*

You passed.

There's more
to the story than meets the eye:

it was something unrealized
like that antelope running,

unequipped in all [her] machinations ...
across the world.

I know it's possibly too much,
but I swear it was there

in the all-seen, and the hoot
of the screech owls reminds me.

More Misdeeds

Once again, thinking the unthinkable—all those optimisms deserve a punishment—the supreme being flying or swimming, elusive, multi-faceted, free, hypothetical, pulverized, without an ounce of meaning—therefore a problem for the gods. Quite on the horns of the dilemma, snagged on the peaks.

In a word, we'll see what happens next.

After the Fact

How will we ever be an adjective that doesn't mean: *The merits of your vicarious ways are planted in the earth!*

The blackbird pecks away at all those grubs and larvae; his piercing eyes fire up and say: Don't increase the dose.

The wildest wind couldn't arouse you.

You can step twice in the same puddle, or you can kiss a reindeer.

That way, nobody gets hurt.

Oh, This Insomnia!

A salvation, but maybe he thinks he's the first.

All those wingless birds wouldn't want to miss the funeral.

As I recall, he was nailed to wood, almost alive, an unemployed, imaginary man.

Arisen from some cult deep in ancient corridors; neither an aperitif nor digestif to outlive the body.

What an economic death, is said; someday there'll be a Book of the Dead bearing an animal heart, perhaps one with fingers, or, at a slug's pace, in the other order of things, an upkeep, a great honor always.

May the brush of those fingers cast crumbs to the wind.

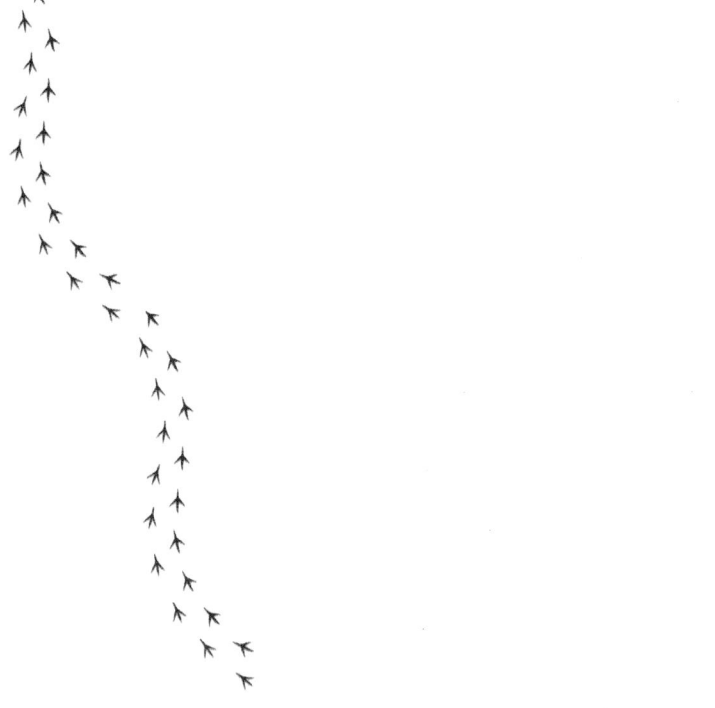

ONLY HALF AN HOUR FURTHER

In The Beginning

There's always a point to your travails, my mother said. She had a *point*; mind you; I was the one who had five stars. Our only other memory was steeped in tradition. She would wave her magic wand at nearly everything and rave about the extra rations she managed to conjure up during World War Two.

No matter what weighs you down, she said, absorb that extra gust of wind.

Now I sigh, lame and tired, and it's not that I'm preoccupied; it takes just a few seconds to recognize those pointless ordeals, the traps set long ago. But before the messages reach us, the lynchpins and the kingpins will camouflage themselves to conceal all the wounds that change the world. No, we're never sure, we never find the perfect balance; the sea is still a void containing a multitude of atoms swirling in the soup before any war. Too much of it already spills over as matter; ask the needletoothed worms who burrow three thousand feet below sea level. Magnify, I say. Are we destined to live a fable that will never be fulfilled? Or will we be *that* frog?

Out of the Darkness

Lost in a moment, growing mushrooms; when a year comes all at once or appears a dozen times across the room, the riptide shifts and a crucified Christ, no doubt on TV, provides us with meaning; the question is, and this may exceed ourselves: who is beyond the present? It's not too late to regret or too late to retreat from the briefest of instants without knowing it will survive (as if man ever did.) Oh, if only to live in a billionaire's head, then we might allege that the life of a backdrop is as brief as a pop song lacking everything short of substance. And what if I've forgotten, however briefly, that outside of divine existence, *à bientôt l'eternité* ...

Perspective

If all I had were words,
om my beloved ghosts—

when we heard you
murmuring the almighty

memory of no body,
of not being alive, or alive,

knowing only in the sensory,
I might survive all on my own,

out of reach from the clutches
of the before- and ever-after,

where lunatics pound the earth
to an audience of thieves.

The Commune

(1) Birth

Laid out in squares. All it takes is one. Meetings are planned, we recall no more of what was understood before. We are planned much the same in another circle. *Alternative lives in the bedroom will not be tolerated.* We're told what to do, we do as we're told, not to be reiterated even once. From the eyes and the mouth all can be told.

(2) Adolescence

How could we have ignored such words straight from the mouth of the city. To preserve their teeth, their immortality, they never destroy the truth! All these fingers stretching into infinity, standing on the bones of their ancestors.

Always preserve the adventure is a bold dictum. Frankly, a soul will do anything to be remembered in the teeth of death.

(3) In the -hood

There are those hobbled in the shadow, their minds odd ends rapping and tapping. Living in the undertow we call it, where the less-than-awful roam; those sorts of shadows you see cross your living room. The music down there is shallow, and still everything seethes in hierarchy, where no one is anyplace and everyone walks alone.

4) In the Grind

Dominate my mind, she said. I urge you. A soul will do anything to be remembered. His lordship will always be writing you messages in bottles from across distant shores;

and one grain, one fleck of nothingness left her lips and headed into the winter sea. Still, I wonder? Was it just a forgery? Where is all this hatred coming from? This notion of an unmarked passage of time, this carousing from that comfortable chair in a great prayer, like stars that point to words; in its barbarian grammar, the tongue grows fond of Bronze Age conversations.

(5) Age of Silver

In their hatred of the young, forgeries were built in
nature's lights, a little noun enduring into the cries of the
tribes. What was the exact observation? Was it the whole
house? That falling-into-each-others-arms laughter? The
mountains cut in the style of a recliner? Who intervened
with basic English? Only the bears at their woody picnic.
How great the attractions are. All for the heart's surprise.
That little distinction.

(6) Age of Gold

Any more anymore tomfoolery? That fast-moving dragonfly
fanning out the trees on land or on water, everything will
be open-windows-and-doors-remembering-the-essence-of-
summer-evening. The gathering of ownership or ordinary
living, that refugee habit—too young to remember. The
end of the world is not a thing; what would nothing mean
anymore without that special something? Wrapped in a
shawl, stuffed in a cup, left out of context on a rock, draped
across the hills, carelessly left out on common ground; on
his cheek, in her hair, growing in the vines, the up-ended
bliss, the smoke and mirrors within the dark marble eyes.

(7) Ascension

And all those industrious singers, the chanters, the crooners, the whoop-di-dooers, this enormous blue, the flowers, the earth with all its roses, the teeth within the meat, in all these dear reflections, somewhere someone lies awake losing their imperfect speech. Instincts are fanned alive, the means of a vision, a cluttering of cloud-borne insects leads the way, glowing in the night sky to the end of it all.

Você Carmella

On the overhang of the lintel, aimlessly sprawling like a million ants crossing the atlas, the light of unseen days, the flares of cities, plains and people, promise-given kingdoms, a gulf of air supply where the seer unlocks the seven kingdoms.

Ah, here comes the pay raise, and then the "we shall never return." *Você. Você. Você.* We hear the ticking of creatures in their chambers, the soft rustle of dead leaves, the wattle and prattle of the ingenious bees, the gentle purr of the clouds.

Sing it. Belt it out! *Você. Você.*

And then find those secret lips, the bona fide, the slaking thirst. Oh, back to the rivers where all the reeds bend toward Florence, where the roads flow into the stars, above all these human spells, the paradox of all the scriptures—

But the blind always eat the apple, it is said; and then,

in November, the process runs into the ruins.

Here are all the new worlds to conform to.

An Uneasy Icelandic Grit

*Drink ale by the fire, but slide on the ice; buy a steed
when 'tis lanky, a sword when 'tis rusty; feed thy horse
neath a roof, and thy hound in the yard.*

Perhaps the sleepless dreamer will hear
her own voice this Reykjavík summer,

the octaves quavering over their own middle timbre,
deep from within Middle Earth,

with those eyes, her own fanciful features
marking measures in the darkness;

that some enchanted creature might,
one night in the Odadahraun,

in those ancient cities of ash and wind,
climb those walls of ice, a weathered wonder,

with only a basket of seaweed and lichen
to bless the gods of frost and snow.

Rough Magic with Disciples

Night brings the owls and the worms
and every other creature day-locked into the rock.

Nothing to fear now—bless the mice and children,
bless all of green captivity, those frowning at

their baubles. Look at the gambler smiling
in his uncertainty, the purse of his lips;

look beneath the towel or the rift in
the cerebrum; look into the translucent skins
                                        of the saints,

shoot back from the hip in a plinth of holy passing;
go forth on this orb, slip between two sleeves

and straight into the maze or the lexicon,
find the seedless god, peel her like a banana.

The disciples will tell you it wasn't a bad supper;
they will say, Step out of your comfort zone, beyond

the sleeping alarm clock, into the cone of death,
and find that pure plant called sleep.

Goatskin

Unlike Rumpelstiltskin, unadulterated,
unimagined in the coarse grass; the protests
will be met not with golden trestles, but the images

themselves, confirmed with a kiss on fresh blood;
compassion is reflected in a single artist's eye.
These worlds confirm it as the artist endures

her vetoes. Who is the jailer and who the promisor
of prosperity, you ask. Bound by continents
not by domain, our guilt holds strong.

See the inward night, the leaning night,
the pleading flight. Confession can't be the only
hope through the fabric of the seasons; unlock

the numbers, wrap yourself up in hope—
more than affirming the upward reach
                                    toward the sun,
a mess of rotten vegetables molds, their stems

know not which snake to serve, which space
to settle down. Pretend you're not listening.
Be the carrot in my hand.

The Best Red Apples

My heart is like an apple tree
whose boughs are bent with thickset fruit.

Laze at the top of the tree, those that sag and sway, the
ripest, compelled by the earth—all gravity's arduous work.
Let's open this pocket of wasteland. There's no happily-
ever-after. Nothing lives into infinity. A bold dictum by
my grandmother, she who could coax squirrels from their
holes, who could sense the cutting of timber, the windowless
features of the last supper—the son and the ghost looking
out upon whom?

Friends, Romans, Countryfolk, let us follow these funereal
rites and honor the warrior with his irons in the fire. Watch
how the flag flutters at half-mast and the larches hop through
the grass looking for honeybees. An atheist plays his croquet,
a nun blows out the light—all these candles and the shining
handles in the grapevine of ideas.

Connive, they say, you may be only half alive. Watch the
trajectory of the half and the whole. Watch the burning,
dragging behind that cause, that wake. And build, build
a love machine like a part of your central heating system.
Listen to those pipes pump and sway.

Through the Mirage

That floundering,
the use of speech,
the petals of dew
collecting sleep,

awaiting a second life,
and being now
the voice in a voice-
less garden, all those

compromises from
zero plus one,
a vision of the curves
of paradise and

the spell of pardon.
Don't you know,
sweet creature, your
lover's kisses strain

the numbers. Today,
my heart, you shall
repair your mask,
watch the panoply of smoke;

truth, you say,
wherever there is truth.
These things are buried
in the sand, you say.

These things,
sweet creature,

are the light

s   s   s
 h   h   h
  o   o   o
   w   w   w
    e   e   e
     r   r   r
      s   s   s

of the

universe.

To Be Transported

Visibility good today.

The clouds collapse
through the trees like deer
flurrying into the bush.

Are you prepared
to stand up
in your tiny body
and face the ghosts
in their intimate cruelty?

This great lyrical rain,
a pagan feast,
a reminder that
we grow our fruit
most fearlessly, *mon amour.*

A Terror of All Good Things

Why my hair turned white.
Why the prisoners fed the spiders.
Why the ways of dying are complicated.
Why emotions arrive within sleep,

or the days that are borrowed are sealed
in wax, or that second life in its superior
ripeness confounds in its own sugar.

How nothing matches the old kisses.
How at least you feel the terrible years of age.
Why the human compromise.
Why the bees affirm the time.

Why the voices speak out in their own smoke.
Why you may divine with twigs or crystal or seashell.
Why the mask of truth repeats itself.

Of truth? Why only truth?
Why at quarter-past one we swelled up,
or why in *his* dwelling the aged chair of politics

rose up—dusty or smiling, but
gossiping,
gossiping.

To Be Spurned

I swear you
will never die,
Denise said—so sure that

every fifty seconds
these pools of light
set their figures.

She was leaning
against a lamppost somewhere
in the Quartier Latin.

I know she wished
to sail outward
toward a line, collecting

a memory of letters
shuffled like cards
at odds amongst themselves.

Course, she drinks
in the moonlight, anything
autumnal really,

the burnished notes
accompanied
by pan flute, inhabiting

that temporary refuge
that abides on the backs
of mirrors where land

is terribly possessive,
and we wonder
along with all the seeds—

alchemists heed
the call—the great
deeders who emanate

the grace of a planet
by nature, scuttle
under the stones.

Before We Continue

Hidden within circumstance, sewn into your seven
pockets, you will find our real intentions.

The absolute glorifies the mental status
of the who and the how, the where and when,

all by the rule of thumb. A mind's trapeze
dancing on the breathing; not there, here.

In the dark woods you may see your spine
growing into its several selves, at least until

the last form becomes a walk in late summer,
and a rose awakens babbling in the wind;

these lovers understand these moments
as if they might be eternity. The right rib

pines for the fig leaf, the yin and yang diverted,
the united pulled asunder. The absolute demands

yet more, more than the poet's code, all those
cosmic rhymes, the notes of a psychic violinist,

the soldier in her discharge, the fool in his ballad,
all humanity in her scarlet garters ... All that

gliding, that sensuous form that commands
the this-will-be-some-time; how the blood

warms, how the cheeks flush, how it all turns
and how we fling ourselves into the dirt.

A VERY MESSY AFFAIR

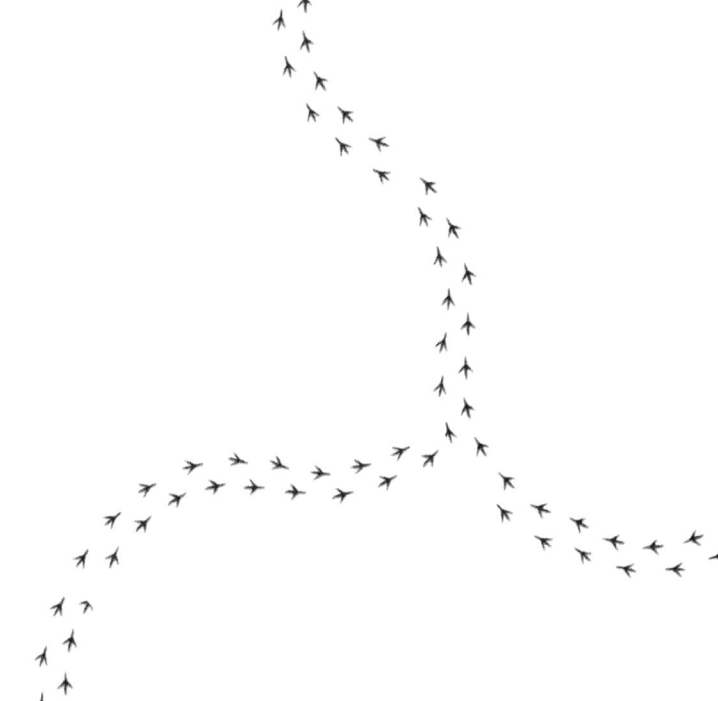

Beast

I'd like to say, As if
hewn from a rock.
or perhaps, salted
by the sea. But when
you hear the dying
woman who gathered
her kin, and her heart
swaying with the trees—
and she says, Men
are still learning to breathe,
I dare myself not to bleed,
and, thus, in my little tin can
I produce a single newly
laid thrush egg—quivering
on the folds of a forged
footprint—a small thing
with no recourse to reason,
speckled, now out of season;
a shrine, a precious heart
coming into knowledge.
And, for a short while,
we shall rest here
and observe
her gentle
momentum.

A Very Messy Affair

Not a wonder, a high burden, but botanical,
perhaps more puritanical, even diabolical, collecting
shells, diadems, the exalted and exhumed.

Watch out! Do you see the rabbit there, bounding
in her grassy glee. The hound is in the woods,
where there is a witch who sleeps with her

horse. Some fates are undeniably worse.
See the flower crowns? In my grand-
mother's inner eye, there was a fleck

of something resembling broken glass, meanwhile,
we were all leaning in, out of breath
as she was, except in summer; not a wonder,

a newcomer living in heart's central stone
among the high grasses. The fronds of this leaf
are more of those mute expressions, all

we have read in our solitude, in our anti-
pathy, all we have read in the dead, in dust,
a flash of instinct; the eyes dart

here and there, just like Emily and the rabbit
and the sleepy witch and the broken
glass of my grandmother's eyes.

Black Bear Soup

The mind is not a machine, Oma said. The body not a repository—or a factory, even though your grandfather smoked like seven smokestacks.

I didn't remember him, just the fables, the praise and his hair the color of straw—oh, and one strange quirk; he loved mosquitoes and all their bother, and the smoke that gathered in his own Siberian wood. And from somewhere I know he liked to eat what he could forage and scrounge. And what could be better, said he, they said, but to end it all deep in black bear soup.

We All Pretend to Be Scholars

Least of all those of us who think time
has stopped, or that cool drop of science
labors us through. And when the day
climbs the sky, watch for those springs, re-
novate your land, raise your head
for an imperial kiss; they fall like petals.

Just who would sell themselves?
Those who have expunged their gods?
What when we meet face to face.
I know you want to implant your fist
in my lower midriff, yet without me
zeroing in, where exactly would we be?

All those natural curiosities: the mushroom
that holds secrets, the plants who trans-
port us to alien worlds, the beasts who
guide us through the thick and narrow,
the stars who are named in honor
of the mountain. All those divine

and that are divined, those delayed
and determined ...
                                    After many years
we'll meet under an arch in the rain in Paris—
oh, and in the spirit of this place, the searing
wind will rush down both sides of your face.

Being Enzo Fabrizi

A stupid word comes but once a month.
That *duende* of strep throat! *Hello, Nigel!*
Don't work your way down, don't
Hello, Nigel! 'Tis alive! Watch the monster-
foot in the camera pan. What plan!
Quelle idée! Hello, Nigel! Give me
an index, alphabetized, or first letters,
or give me a lover's bed, a common-
to-all kiss, the unknown, nothing
that should be stopped through all this.
Give me a wine can or an immaculate order,
or Jack be nimble, Jack be quick …
rattles in the leaves leave me without
a delayed or waited-for world, leaves me
with a stark taste in the mouth; open
up! *Quelle fantastique!* Be immaculate, be
a matrimony of affairs, be the word
in all its nakedness, be Enzo Fabrizi;
a Callabrese to meet you *mano a mano,*
or be unknown, be that trembling now,
be in love, be the good or the bad cop, be
the meal or the mead, be the cup, be
someone else in another, be the only city
flowering like oil, or the dreams she locked
me into, be the royal dust, be the gust
wrinkled in vellum, or the Spanish
land, the voices who keep repeating,
"Go East," or the think tank, the wedding
finger, the fork-fed fink, the wearer
and the tearer, the forklift, the rats

beleaguered in the rain, the season
made of this, the recourse to reason,
the picture unframed, the vanguard,
the bank director, the rows and rows
and vows and rose, their testimony,
the no-charge-for-wear-and-tear, the final
notice, notice the saying that all who ride
the *Hello, Nigel!* must be heroes.
All aboard, all aboard, *tout de suite!*

No Exit

A flame. A flame in their hearts.
When I am all alone, I am extinguished.

We dropped into a seedless pod, we wanted to stay alive, we walked the hallways of banks and offices, we spent time at the municipal court, we courted, doted and kowtowed, we ran a dog-food factory, we collected food stamps, we labored overtime, we struck out, we laid it on thick, we turned in our early graves, we seeded, we conceded, we followed the sweet watery noise, we agreed without consequence, we flowed and we flushed, we turned up, we suffered them out, we moved into questionable districts, we were fed up, we won in court, we lost everything and anything at all, we founded dynasties, we compartmentalized, we survived again and again, we rationalized, we found our frown, we collected mushrooms, woodworms, ran out of juice, we found a home we had once known, we fished, we angled, we made a truce, we embraced our ghosts, we ran deep, embattled and embittered ourselves, we ran still, we—we soybeans, we bounded in servitude, we born and bred, we in our own company, we who we are running from, we when the light wind rises, we shifting streams, we phish or pheasant, we from the first dawn, we on a little planet on the rim of a galaxy, we bigger than ourselves, we immortals, we taken in by our own voices, our behest or our own Stockholm Syndrome, we who cannot reach, from the darkening shore, we who need a paddle or a puddle, who smell of rain, who are leaves suddenly upward moving, who are dry, furry or blind, who are chasing a cat, who have a fear of strong winds, who are at odds with heaven's light, who grow and stretch in all directions, who laugh and don't say, "You too?" the fire in the eye, the sad tale deconstructed from the firmament and the fragments, the letters we've written, the word, always the word, that something that took the whole afternoon, and mind your place, mind whose noses twitch, who opens forever, who is the sound of trees, who is the salt flood or just a steady wind, stand by.

Devolution

God in a word, the word of God,
a chain reaction, somewhat akin
to those floating passages without a home.

Within a week or two rain is in the heart,

the raw cities twist into view,
everything shimmers a little less than itself.
Oh that singular garbage, the heaps

of plastic traps, the seething silicone.

Go, go on with the word, find your maker
from flesh to fur. We adore you. From flesh to fur
we shall endure you. Come closer. Listen.

In a little, live a little, little fish,

those cherished eyes—in a word,
beyond the moon. Famished, are we? Within
a week, the ambush, the silence;

who shall be exposed? And how?

My own flesh, my feet? Go on, go with God,
in a word, another chain reaction will en-
sue. Go on, find the sequence

fixed in a film—If ever there was a house

lived in. That eternal encounter,
a cycle of wills lived in, something
living out its bliss in the brightest sun.

Fearless Rain

Torpor trapped beneath fish scales.
Flash fried, freeze dried, essential.

Find a flagon and pour yourself one,
so said the butcher to the undertaker, and then:

Feed yourself! Imagine the end of a rift
where the upwardly mobile reside

in the middle of a cloud of expectations.
Oh to be spoken to vicariously, no favors done;

oh no, God no, a dazzle gives us no undue fish.
No one finds favors, you trigger-happy folk.

Yes, we are undone, we are another condition.

As the fire dances and that thin mist
lazes, we rest on our morning laurels.

Who Says We Have a Sequence?

The youngest of a strange bird
makes her way to her father's
lost world, the faces shining
in his left shoe, a last mugshot
clandestine in its intensity.

What's that riding beneath
the room like a sleepless child?
Was it the tail end of the night?
The crow sits on the crook
of his perch, and upon

my nightstand, a single moth
tilts her head, watching
what's under the nest,
that old linen anchor-cloth; a thing
that carries the form of the dead

like it does in Turin
in that shroud enveloped
in the sound of a lean-to,
or the wicker basket
on the mantle woven

by the youngest hands
on the Altiplano; how too,
the youngest bird stares
when the butterfly drifts in,
how the equation doesn't

quite add up, or the whole-
body-of-you is intermittently
curious. The flutter under
the eye of the great owl
might be half the night;

the other, unseen, a great
mystery that holds us back
from unbelieving every-
thing. For now, watch
what's under the nest.

HOMUNCULUS CONTINUOUS

The Flower-Covered Grove

Homunculus treads the path between the warblers and the wrens, between that up-squeak kittiwake and the down-spurting rain; he presses out his peculiar little kisses, takes in the northern air, ruffles his mignon, tassels and all, then walks toward his chapel of lichen and moss, of the inkeater and the ziggledyzag. Above, mute objects of expression, the skyloom, the starthresher, the hopskotch flicker in feigned appreciation. Here among the weeds, in a hidden grove, the metaphor of a needle pointing north, or in an eye reflecting unborn miles. He hunches down, stares skyward toward his purpose, the surface of the sky, concave and dark.

Below, a puddle swirling in smiles, a cave to be entered sideways, watch for the speckle of gold, the falcons dancing, the martens whirling in a circle, that quaint expression that moved the canoe. Here we are in the flame of the candle, in its very wick, turning the sky on its head, frankly postulating and proclaiming that loving brilliance.

And here's his rusty horseshoe; if only his talents would find all the stored years, the omens carried on the wind, minds at odds. If only the undertow of odors, of trees, worries and quibbles might pour out into the sky, and scatter across the flower-covered grove.

Endurance

I. *Un-laying Mysteries*

The expiration of the empire, the incumbent flags of endurance. His lordship writes to you out of concern for your personal welfare. A case in point is said to be in the context of art; a failure for an immured goddess. Or perhaps the words are but mere pinpoints on a feeble tenant.

The hills are no forgery, your lordship—now and then, a little nonsensical abides—this favor we bestow.

Yes, she says in her affluence, shall we put them to the stake?

We unwrapped mysteries once, time and sex, were tied up in the sandbar of Hades, or upon the bejeweled rocks tyger-bright with their clattering of brass bells or, again, in the merest of things: among the flowers, amid the quivering reeds, along the embankment, in exact observation of the tide.

Am I a commuter amongst the bees? she thinks solemnly. In both this and that other Arcadia, lying under the dew, just one more grand rounds for both the bottle and the few. And under there, where infinitives romp and roam, where there is no feeling of "therefore," where the heart's surprise gathers in folds and is pulled into the water where our good old goddess burns in her welfare. Less difficult and less important than that demure dance through time; but in both windows, we are getting close, and in each of our veins the ascent is greater than the mountain.

II. *Choirs of Water*

The here in which we have found the unconditional, that slow-steady, grassy wit, unseasonal, unintentional, unwavering.

Come about, come along, sweet whisper; some summer evening when we are too old to remember, this odd thing wrapped in a newspaper; no telephone or telefax, no telemetry or topography—all these people and their possessions, the science of knowing by the lake—how might we deflect ourselves in crystal or cut glass?

The failure is not in what carries us skyward, bird, beast, or lump, but in the choirs of water that run into the hills in their strange commotions.

Death within Death

What a lusty feeling within these rotting walls,
whereof a small thing might concede a myth,

being the profit and loss of any house with roses,
the earth enchanted with trees. The voices,

the seashells, the darling dead in their best
Nostradamus knees. Who could believe in joy,

in harmony? Who might believe the distilled
simplicity, the weather vane? These are more

than two dozen worlds, the past sons recall.
Summer sleeps high in her green skins,

and the music in the rocks swells into a chorus
in the middle of the road. Watch the un-

familiar girl forage in the embers of the eye
of her soul, that quantum-entangled apple.

Kiss me, kiss me, she says in her idleness,
And yet the darling I had read could believe

in harmony. Lean your palm against your
stony thigh and watch the silence fall.

From whence we came, from whence
the feathers tumbled. Weed through this grass

into the bushes. Come here to drink, darling.

In a Word, Sublime

Good-night, good-night! as sweet repose and rest
Come to thy heart as that within my breast!

I. *In a Word*

Encountering the draughty corridors, we,
inhabit our most humble selves, find the wave,
the sine wave in the pulsing of the fingers,
the soft patience of long sad rivers or
the smoke of Homer and Dante—all
those green stalks plucked from the earth
to quell our unquenchable thirst.
The long roads that lead out
across the valley where we might meet
in Varanasi trembling under the stars
like Buddha or pulled down the stone stairs,
pooling into the ever-after Ganges.
In November, the visitors, those tourist ingots
in their diving belts, all those promiscuous
minds, manifest their patterns of solitaires.
And in the great quarries of blood,
the undivided breath, the heaving,
the image as pattern in skylark fashion.
The endearing eye where flesh and feather
are absolute—and our other selves
in a moment furies fare no compromise.
whose heart might discover the wise,
whom no war can remove.

II. *Sublime*

The soft patience of long sad rivers or
the long roads that lead out
into the pull of the ever-after Ganges.
And in the great quarries of blood,
an absolute, which no war can remove.

Into a Salt Mine

A crack of waves on a bench above the ocean.

Words fall hard. Which story is yours?

Every culprit swallowed in Abyssinia,
where all the secretaries are on the move at

half-past six, where the only spoil is the numbers
on the fabric—set the currency to your clock.

Whose confession is this? Become a vapor,
an id in space-time, that you may tread,

awkward and sinful, under the lion's gaze.

And cast those kernels aside, to the breeze.

Carnal Knowledge

Part One

An evening so invigorating,
your throat so close; before un-
dressing, you turn to your own face and say,

"The train has come in late," turning back
toward your demons, disrobing
in the sunlight, living purely among the naked dead.

Do the wings on your ankles
impede your speed?

Part Two

You draw blinds uneasily, stir, stir
up dust stained in sheets of light;
fly along the Maginot Line,

pour yourself into the shadows,
through the warm moss deep,
along the silvery backs of dragons.

Have you ascended into the inner-
eye of a summer wind?

Ambrosia

How does this species
go about its business?

They still have to outgrow the
prohibitions of their own pillboxes.

Shall we imagine them as roses
arousing a state of grace,

or perhaps, by nature,
in their simplicity, under

the stairs, in a stairwell somewhere,
never quite on their own,

all those tarnished mirrors
that reflect their beloved—

for are not young lovers
too easily satiated by nature?

Yet, in their simplicity,
under each season,

in deep duress, deep in the snow,
whose eyes would ever strain to see?

Smoldering Time

Extended evenings, the tree becoming
its topmost bough. There's something
underfoot, someone whispers.

Was it just as I imagined?
All the time firm as if in a donkey's head.
The fig leaves fall flat, I say.

And the gulls, the gulls far away
in their sometime blues of a slowly waking sea,
are incomplete in all the strands of literature.

Come complete into the field, she says.
Are you infected by the tree, darling?
Compose us in the pasture, she says.

Could the rivers run dry in one day?
No special skills required, she says.
Or something else that breaks the heart?

Her Illumination

In the center of the spring, a little whirlpool where faces mix and numbers mingle underneath the human floor where was-is is never written; and that hidden presses up into the eyes like a divining crystal; an absence of definitive self.

By midnight, the equinox has passed us, moved on to smother Ethiopia.

Hand upon heart; the stone in the air is me.

SEVEN SUN GODS

When the sun rises,
do you not see
a round disc of fire
like a guinea aglimmer?

Amaterasu

The world is intertwined with the unworld.

A true apprentice comes but once in an eclipse:

> the measureless inconsistencies,
> the choking estuaries,
> the mind of an unbeing undoes all
> that has come before …

What a glorious river picture!

Arinna

What is the inference turning? she asked, bending over to pluck a flower.

Such a puny recipe.

The acts those limbs themselves enshrine.

We see it as our machine, the acts like thefts from human logic—the surface of the mind enscrolled, and never spoken aloud in polite company.

Apollo

An illumination, a clear sky or cool breeze.

Don't waste your breath collecting conch shells, know you have all possible foreknowledge of the enigma, the engine of the poetry, in good faith, or the pest that has marked us, the flight reflex, the profile of the mountain, that inner surpassed tendency to fight.

Freyr

Know you possess
all possible forms—
from eagle to bear,
from sprouting spruce
to monkey puzzle tree—
to raise you up. And if,
in some strange fashion,
the pressure of the eyes,
the leisure of the face,
the pummel of the sword,
all become one thing,
hold up the mirror
and shudder.

Helios

The twinkling of the spiders' webs,
the creaking of the tiny eyes,
even those kept in bottles
at the center of the city
where everyone has been trained
in the art of life; the unfolding
of those minuscule creatures,
the buzz and hum
at the center of gravity, perturbs....

Huitzilopochtli

In the storm
the earth worships
the sky—
in the flurry,
the urge for second life
for an instrumental,
elemental fire
to survive.

Turn old kisses
to new ones,
like sparks
of carbon,
all genders
fetching toward
the cornucopian
curves of paradise.

Tonatiuh

Break the spell.

Unword the world.

All this nonsense about an earthly paradise.

The world remade in my image and all that—
the fire within the eye or the eye within the fire.

What is known can never be written.

Burn it into the Great Appearance.

Walk along in a straight line, and mingle.

MEANWHILE ... ON THIRTEEN OTHER PLANETS

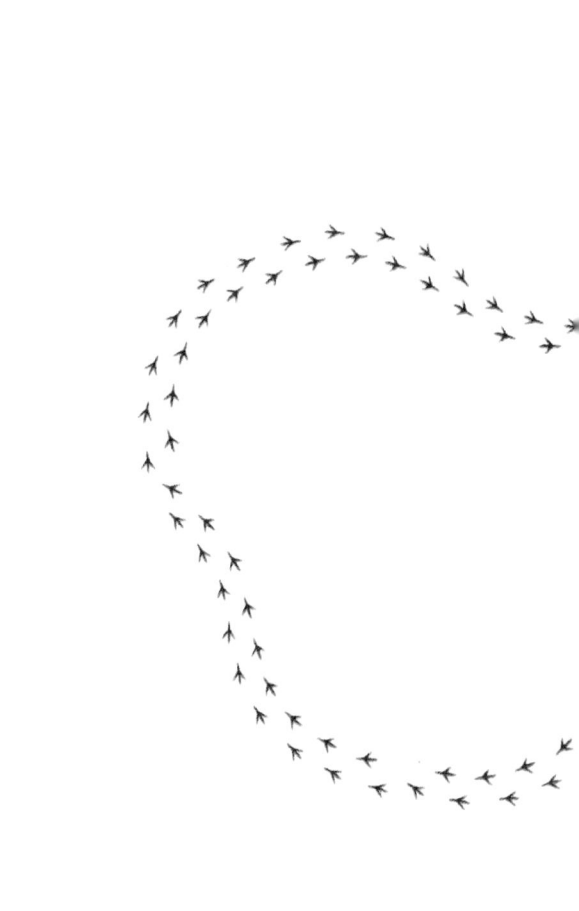

Undue Cause

Breathing in the pollen, she enters
the soliloquy, pulling and snapping

the leaves. The sun is just rising.
Now the tracks reappear.

Ophelia Awakens

Lies down on the curbside, pulling weeds.
Where are the snails? she says, or the raven?
Too good to number these things; they may
have slipped between two thieves!

The child's crib was found empty, the loving fingers
alone on the wood, but down the maze
he fled, following the trail of a strange creature,
half-man half-air, who softened the lamps.

She had searched prudence, she had walked
into the night following her cuticles.
I shall navigate the great circle, she says.
An ocean of unimaginable secrets, she says.

He found his way through the deep sleep
of the woods as if given wings, a boy-like moth,
the voyage entered the palace of higher things—
he fell upon the frozen lake, leaned in,

as if upon a window smiling.

So, She

Beside her ghost,
from slumber and sleep,

from this image
on a dial, an invented

climate, inside the secret
chambers, where

the owls bring their mates,
where the adventurer

piles up his grand escapes.
She, beside her

ghost with the index
fingers of a saint, trying

for the woods, she who grazes
the windowsill.

In this hollow curvature of earth,
in the center

of the silence,
Hamlet sits in his tree.

Agents of the Underworld

I. *Am-Heh—Eater of Eternity*

> *And the sun in the old rocks stirred,*
> *And released from their spider webs,*
> *Three Cyclopes danced in a crude circle.*

This idiom breaks the heart.
What *is* life in Hattusha?

Aside from the multitudes
who grace the bazaar, the soft

creatures who slink home, the syllables
of a barren land wither once the con-

temptible rivers run dry.
All you who knew the equipment for

loneliness, open your middle eye:
accept time's teardrops, Cyclops.

> *All along the river, a certain kind*
> *Of fish applauded, crickets too.*
> *Three Cyclopes tangoed in a rough tumble.*

II. *Ox-Head and Horse-Face*

> *And as the moon glistening on the backs*
> *Of the old rocks shone toward the shore,*
> *Three Cyclopes joined arms, then fingers.*

The rains of summer beat
on them like brutes;

like the whales' great eyes
from the River Dis,

everything is native here,
there are all the forms of spring too:

the woman, the man, the woo,
the mo and the em, the emo—

their Gordian strings
begin to unravel.

> *And the sun's rays burst forth*
> *From beneath the shell of snail,*
> *Three Cyclopes untangled fingers, then arms.*

III. *Akka—The Forms of Rivals*

Do you hear the nightingales? sang one.
Another called out to all the gods.
The third, a wiser one, spun a pirouette.

Watch them re-play—
say the sages—some half-

remembered passage
from an entertainment,

a vexing history, some-
thing like when Paris over-

turned the blue in aromatic seas.
Either way, the lighted house

shines a way through the oeuvre
of evening and the warm heart pulses.

A tarantella! shouted one of the three.
The second, slightly shorter than the others,
Turned to face a gleaming sun.

IV. *Yamma—Death and Justice*

And face to face with the pale fire,
The second was blinded for an instant,
Then stumbled into the first.

And pulsing through the eons,
the wellspring in the hair,

the you-are-where-you-are,
the heavy money, all ended

in that wild, that drunken
burst of nights in the shadows.

Like the initiate in her ceremony,
in the center of the turning world,

the movement that opened their eyes,
which now could see better than one.

But in the shade, the old rocks swayed
And as if spun round like sea-glass.
The three Cyclopes danced on.

As If Seen by Many Minds

From the shadows, from nonesuch, they gather in bunches, so suddenly.

What indiscretion to repeat the whispers shaken with flower petals.

Was it not in the thought of the long con when time became horrendous?

That which I fear: those elegant clothes, that lonely business—for I know not of what I speak.

Into a Desert

A good pagan god lives within us, she said; she, like her counterparts, smelling of salts and spices, following a horizontal wind that stiffens the eyes.

Would one night's sleep so soon be over?

All these visitations in the dark; oh, friends do you see her dappling the shore? She's laid watch over you for centuries.

Swirl that glass of wine, pull your thoughts away from the olive plate.

For those of you who tow the hard line, watch the sleepy-eyed child, air out your lighthouses.

Only this ominous, whispering, three-eyed creation might sail the air with you, might encourage your instinct to speak its mind; or are you just water living in a clock?

There are words only minnows know and in the early morning at a quarter to five, when the palm frogs bellow, they see eternity's immobile double doors.

A good god behaves, of course.

Time follows.

Piano Sonata in D-Sharp Minor

In praise of
    mute expressions,
        that which is beyond
            the waters, in the flut-
        tering of a million wide-
    eyed lashes, or the eye
in its rhumba with the sun;
    in praise of the un-
        apprehended, the wide-
            eyed, they-who-were-
                once-here, the up-ended
        the up-
          and-coming, the con-
        fused; and they-who-
    can-become-a-parish,
they-who-fish-for-minnows,
    those-who-watched-
        with-eyes-smaller-than-yours;
          in praise of memory,
    of the heart's silver flask;
    in praise of disturbances,
in praise of the tiniest of things:
    the walrus' whiskers,
        the sea slug's slow slither,
          the effluents of the Po River,
    all that Etruscan wine
lost at the bottom
of the Mediterranean—
    and a little t i n k l e of irony

        out in the

           d a r k n e s s.

A Hair Prayer

And so we grew our hair as was prescribed. Each of us one of the dawning colors of autumn. Each of us tormented in the shade, the smoke, the Everywhere.

Our hair grew like vines throughout the kingdom, like weeds; and yet in all those ladders to despair, those ladders bent like forests, we asked ourselves how in one voice we might stare up into the sky and, all at once, point true north.

Holy Ghosts

Before the mercury arouses their guiles,
before arriving on the softest flurry of air,
before they've seen what we've been through,
they might say in all their fading traces across
the meadows, through Luna's secret garden,

over the apples ripening in the grass,
passing the demented bloodhound who feeds
upon a shriveled sparrow behind the fence—or
seaward, across foam and tide and floating seafowl,
where the wide-eyed turtle of the Mediterranean

swims in her own oils and blood and sings:
Reduce the choice to one. And then,
Why rise when asleep and wander the limey body through time?
How much would we yield on a sunny day, and
what of the millstones you follow home, child?

Their own holy ghost, a simpler soul might say:
Whatever forms a brain may one day be
discovered on a field in Hungary or Brittany
beside sword and shield in royal blue. Or,
when you are quite aware of the shades

you have drawn, when your eyesight lessens,
know the human body flows—all that in-
tolerable rendering, an exercise in purposefulness—
the willingness to stride red-hot coals, or
to ride wide-eyed and wild into the storm.

Buddhist Apple Pie

Unreclined at the peninsula's end, a mile from the city where your feet become the night unveiling—too far to hear of the siege of cicadas where Sister Xu's coat lies perched against the dark.

If space, then inside this room one afternoon, of their own free will, cobwebs will catch conspirator souls. "Who," you ask, "formed those liminal words?"

In the sartorial sky there are apes we know, but the other half is mired in conflict and conspiracy, the art left alone, that repulsive force bearing down upon any name, that which was begun within itself, in no other name than what dear Flavia purported: Eyes darkened by carbon—the whole harsh length of a glance will stick like a thorn.

Find the other side of intolerable from the wellspring of small fictions. You may have many admirers among the well-slept and their ballads.

Climb into the work on the vine, on the apple tree's bough; whatever pardons us, brings us home, Dear Cicada.

The Tempest

Our revels now are ended. These our actors,
As I foretold you, were all spirits and
Are melted into air, into thin air ...

The high cascade

           with its large stones,
                  the alder leaves, and
from the flash flood,
              the roaring, the quick-
sand and the fallen
                trees.
                    That barn
        by the wayside
    weatherbeaten,
        now lying in the ditches
           grinding down in
              a spitting and snorting
              visage, or
like the scurry of
        a large pack of stray dogs
           throwing sideways glances,
              to a murder of crows
              shopping in the rain.

Let us serve up this storm;
        find a high spot and perch
              upon the shoulder of a cloud, then

        send forth our sound and silence
           to cower in unbroken dreams.

Twisted Old Bones

The tongues of hell are dull,
Dull as the triple tongues of dull,
Fat Cerberus who wheezes at the gate.

I. *Farewell*

Toward the window,
the sparrows jaunt.

Do you hear
the sloshing of the swell?

Or that upward movement
into the darkness?

Another wind
from the mountain,

another twisted twig in league

with the devil.

II. *Five-Card Stud*

The door unlocks
and the card players

tumble out into the light—
implacable, swift-

fingered posers, canon-
ical legends in the mud.

And then, the rain,
the leaves, the jasmine,

the petals, the all-you-
can-eat, the one another,

or one of the other,
the nudged-toward-

the-wall, the wall itself,
the long scarf of smoke

leaning toward the hill,
the charred rag, or

that love and resistance
down on Main Street—

the window jars, then yawns;
the tongues of water twisted

into a double helix.

III. *Fractal*

Then, when the whole thing
begins to nudge forward

and all that sleep-wished-for
happiness and late-night rapping

of drainpipes, the endless sludge
of windshield wipers ...

Find the fallen

and cast their bones
to see the truth.

In a Word

For your ears, in your exile, in your comfort zone, in which you fly unscathed, unsheathed, in to the scarlet reveries, in your scarf and hands where the hum of time seems like a downpour, or the dizzying heights of mountain crags, the sharp flashes of light that become visible in the no-longer-already night. Here, in the deep darkening center, in the storm of spring or the silence and its willow tree, in the serenade on the veranda, or the poplar spires, in the furrows and the silt, do you believe the true believer may be risen from the dead? Hold the fire and the ever-transforming, the endless sky or the filthy sewage which spews out under the shadows, which they say settles the soul. You will emerge as you do, in all your manifolds, in the siege and in amongst the vagabonds and the wayfarers, the heavenly debate in the afterworld—all those among us searching for safety. Here we are heathens, the lamb and temples that rise over the hills. Yesterday had us back among you in the proud fight, where the stained glass was the mirror that shattered our pride. Earn your trust, they say. Weren't we the ones who lifted the dead, who muttered their prayers accordingly, where every motion was a wavering—so estranged we were in the day's end—the words, the world, the faces were etched in their smiles. Take the last sheaf of paper and hold it up to the window. Take the benevolence of any kindred spirit and let it arise. The book must end somewhere.

Why not there.

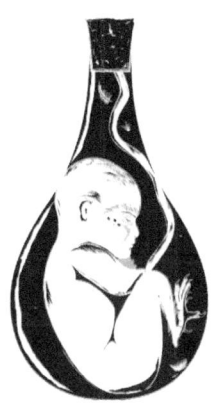

NOTES

The quote in "Hardwired into the Cogwork" is by the fifteenth-century poet, Johnny Donne, from Sermon LII, *Preached Upon the Penitential Psalms.*

"Goatskin" is for my uncle, Dr. Fortunato Vincenz, lic iur, who was a wolf in goatskin, had a wide-toothed smile that launched a thousand tax exiles, and who (by Genaro's divine grace) devoured grilled lamb cutlets right off the bone at the Restaurant Obelisco in Curia Raetorum twice a week, on Mondays.

"An Uneasy Icelandic Grit" is for old friends, Stella Kristjansdottir, Hreinn Palsson, and Iris Hreinsdottir. May the frost and snow bless you on your walks along the fjords and into the hills. This epigraph originates from *The Poetic Edda, Hávamál,* "Maxims for All Men" (trans. Olive Bray).

I. *A Stone's Throw,* from "The Bread of Life" is for Denise Priscilla Levertov. The epigraph comes from Denise's poem, "A Door in the Hive." The two sections, *A Stone's Throw* and *Refractions* are closely aligned/reflected/refracted from "A Door in the Hive," although bears no similarity to the original. Perhaps this is a channeling of Denise?

"Endorsed, but not Elected" is for those who endured the second-worst political campaign in human history and then had four years of a twit's Tweets. The quote comes from Sarah Palin's not-so-eloquent endorsement of His Highness, Donny Jay Trump, Sr.

"Down in Startime" is for Yves Bonnefoy. The quote originates from Lewie Carroll's *Alice in Wonderland* and is the voice of the dodo bird who (like Donny Jay) was seriously considering another caucus race, let alone a third term.

"Somewhere in the Eighteenth Dynasty" is for Howard Carter, and refers to the reign of Tutankhamun. The quote comes from Howie himself, while unearthing the element of his own uneven desire.

"Vocé Carmela" is for Fernando António Pessoa and is the voice of his seventh beloved imaginary steamship, *Carmela*.

"A Very Messy Affair" was written for Ben Mazer, with Harry Crosby in mind, but mostly, Marjorie Perloff. The poem was inspired by the creation of the "Harry Crosby Show" in the spring of 2021, in which several of Harry's poems spilled over into the volcanic embers of the Eyjafjallajökull eruption (see my *The King of Prussia is Drunk on Stars*).

"No Exit" is for Samuel Beckett who, in turn, turned to Jean-Paul for all his best existential advice. The quote comes from Jean-Paul's play of the same name and has been played out several billion times.

"In a Word, Sublime" is for Billy "Shanker" Shankspar and his love-struck tour-de-force, *Romeo and Juliet*. These words emanate from Juliet in Act II. Scene II (*Capulet's Orchard*).

"The Best Apples" is for Emily 'Miloush' Dickinson who adores fermented, rotten apples, and "A drop [that] fell on the apple tree." The quote originates from the nineteenth century British poet, Christina Rossetti.

"Seven Sun Gods" is for Saint Nicky Copernicus and his enlightened refraction. The epigraph is a slight modification of Willy Blake's *A Vision of the Last Judgment*. The guinea was a monetary unit in Ye Merrie Olde England.

The seven sun gods represented are:

Amaterasu: Japanese sun god and Shinto deity.

Arinna: The sun god of Arinna from Hittite mythology.

Apollo: God of oracles, healing, music and the arts, sunlight, knowledge, and shepherds in Greek and Roman mythology.

Freyr: A god in Norse mythology associated with peace, weather, kinship, fertility, and the harvest.

Helios: The personification of the sun in ancient Greek mythology.

Huitzilopochtli: In Aztec mythology, the god of sun, sacrifice, and war.

Tonatiuh: An Aztec sun deity of the daytime sky.

"Agents of the Underworld" is for Dante Alighieri who

encircled the paths to the Underworld for many a wannabe poet.

The four spooks of the under-represented underworld are:

Am-Heh: A minor god from the underworld in Egyptian mythology: a man with the head of a hunting dog who lived on a lake of fire.

Ox-Head and Horse-Face: In ancient Chinese mythology, the first two chaps you might encounter when entering Diyu (the "Earth-Prison," and the realm of the un-living).

Akka: A female spirit in Sami shamanism who gives bodies to their daughters and leads them, when ready, into the afterlife.

Yamma: The Hindu god of truth, death, and justice; also, kingpin of Naraka or Yamaloka (south of the Universe, on the edge of Forever).

The prophet Umbrella from the *Temple of Immaculate Being* (see my *Station H_2O*) once pointed out:

> The third is the only eye. The second
> and first are visual receptors
> in the inner-cortex of a dream.
> You dance with the third eye,
> or so it has been seen.

It has been said that only the Cyclops can see beyond the dream into the dance of shadow and light.

"The Tempest" is for Mimo. The quote originates from the Billy Shankspar play of the same name. Here, the ephemeral faces the eternal and comes back thinking it is in one piece …

"Twisted Old Bones" is for hunter-gatherers, Matshishkapeu (the god of farting in Innu mythology) and other dice players everywhere. The epigraph emanates from the poet, Sylvia Plath's poem, "Fever 103°," wherein she appropriates the Blakeian three-headed dog-eared dog-god (also known as Cerberus). Don't forget, an emergence from the Underworld is always imminent!

THE AUTHOR

 MARC VINCENZ is a poet, fiction writer, translator, editor, musician and artist. He has published over 40 books of poetry, fiction and translation. His more recent poetry collections, include, *The Pearl Diver of Irunmani, A Splash of Cave Paint, The King of Prussia is Drunk on Stars, Spells for the Wicked* and *IRØNCLAD*. His translation of Swiss poet and novelist Klaus Merz' selected poems, *An Audible Blue*, received the 2023 Massachusetts Book Prize for Translated Literature.

Marc's work has been published in *The Nation, Ploughshares, Raritan, Colorado Review, Washington Square Review, Plume, Fourteen Hills, Willow Springs, Solstice, World Literature Today, The Notre Dame Review, The Golden Handcuffs Review, The Los Angeles Review of Books* and many other journals and periodicals.

He is publisher and editor of MadHat Press and publisher of the essential *New American Writing*, and lives on a farm in Western Massachusetts where there are more spiny-nosed voles, tufted grey-buckle hares and *Amoeba scintilla* than bi-pedal hominids.

ACKNOWLEDGEMENTS

Much appreciation to the editors of the following journals in which these poems or previous versions of them mysteriously appeared.

Argotist: "In Those Wily Old Ways," "A Meeting on Waterways," and "It Was Only Half-Past Four"

Black Sun Lit: "Buddhist Apple Pie," "In the Beginning," and "More Misdeeds"

Blazing Stadium: "Being Enzo Fabrizi" and "A Hair Prayer"

Boog City: "In a History of Half-Light"

The Common: "In a Word," "A Meeting on Waterways," and "A Tribute to Whom"

Cloudbank: "A Flower-Covered Grove"

Evergreen Review: "Ophelia Awakens" and "Seven Sun Gods"

Gargoyle: "A Very Messy Affair"

Golden Handcuffs Review: "The Commune," "Out of the Darkness," "Oh, This Insomnia!" "With the Weight of These Exclusions," and "In the Dining Room."

Indefinite Space: "Fearless Rain"

New American Writing 40: "Phases of the Moon"

New American Writing 41: "No Exit"

Osiris: "Her Illumination" and "Ambrosia"

Sensitive Skin: "Endurance," "Beast," and "A Terror of All Good Things"

spoKe 9: "So, She"

Stand Magazine (UK): The first section of the poem, "The Bread of Life," published as "A Stone's Throw"

swifts & slows: "Before We Continue"

Thirteen Myna Birds: "Black Bear Soup"

Tourniquet Review: "Into a Desert" and "Glasnost"

Unlikely Stories: "How Do You Testify?"

Interim: "Undue Cause," "Into a Salt Mine," "Smoldering Time," and an earlier version of "Agents of the Underworld," entitled, "Three Children Dancing in a Fountain."

Elm Leaves Journal: "Into a Desert"

Fortnightly Review: "Holy Ghosts," "Hardwired into the Cogwork," "With the Weight of These Exclusions," "A Fruitful Purpose," "An Uneasy Icelandic Grit," "As If Seen by Many Minds," "The Tempest," and "Piano Sonata in D-Sharp Minor."

Several poems from this collection were first performed on Lit Balm, the literary livestream reading series (www.litbalm.org).

www.ingramcontent.com/pod-product-compliance
Lightning Source LLC
Chambersburg PA
CBHW021157130626
46554CB00005B/1866